Copyright © 2025 Kevin Marlow

All rights reserved

No part of this book may be reproduced, or stored in a retrieval system, or transmitted in any form or by any means, electronic, mechanical, photocopying, recording, or otherwise, without express written permission of the publisher.

ISBN: 9798306485775

Editor: Kevin Marlow
Cover design by: Kevin Marlow

Printed in the United States of America

Contents

Copyright	
Jenny's Biography	1
Budget Book	3
World of Poetry Award 1	7
World of Poetry Award 2	8
Sacrifice of a Mother	9
How Thankful We All Should Be	10
A Loved One You Can Hold	12
Blue Pigeon	14
One Family One Earth	16
Binitos	18
When I Was Young	20
Christmas 1972	21
Hopeless Situation	23
Michelle	24
Beans in the Field	26

A Poem About Spring	28
The Seasons	30
My Dearest Husband	32
Father	33
A Valentine to My Husband	34
To My Husband	36
May I Live Each Day	37
Over Forty	38
No Stars at Night	40
One Long Curse	41
God's Eyes	43
Timmy Lee	45
Thorns in Our Crown	47
As I Lay Sleepless	49
This Is My House	51
Happy Father's Day	53
Waiting is Never Over	56
Fall	58
Travel	59
What if	60
Over the Hill Gang	62
Bowling	63
The Sweet Hearts	64
The Devil Has Been Loosed	65

Here for a Little While	67
Like a Cancer	68
I Pray I Go Quick	70
I Leave My Love	72
No Fancy Casket	74

Jenny's Biography

Genevieve Mae Pate was born August 11, 1923 in Weaver, Williamson County, IL. Weaver was a coal mining town North of Herrin, IL. The workers lived in a settlement near the mine. The miners' children attended a school built by the mine and families shopped at a company store. According to the Williamson County Historical Society, a fire in 1930 burned 17 houses and left half of the population homeless. By 1938, the mine shut down, and Weaver was abandoned and sold by the mining company.

In one of the last conversations with Babe, as her boys called her, she told me that after her Dad lost his job at the mine, her parents, and siblings: Evelyn, Emma Lou, Patricia, Juanita, and Earl Sr. were allowed to live in a corn crib by a doctor who owned a farm. They eventually settled in Ferges, Williamson County, IL, known as Fudge Town by the residents.

They were very poor and subsisted on what work their Dad, Freeman Pate, known as Papaw could find and his occasional bootlegging. Her Mom, Mary Pate (Beasley), known to the family as

Meemaw, grew a garden and canned food to provide for her children.

Genevieve married Angelo Marlow (Merlo), and lived as a homemaker for the three boys they raised together, Larry, Gary, and Paul. Angelo drove a truck delivering beer and liquor for Southern Illinois Wholesale, located behind what is now S.I. Bowl in Carterville. Jenny had many Grandchildren, Great Grandchildren, Nieces and Nephews. More than a Mother, she wrote poetry. This book is a collection of her poems.

Rather than tell you who she was as a person, I want her words to tell you. These poems were saved from a hand-typed diary in a form most today would call journaling. She submitted her poetry for publication, and received Honorable Mention Awards for two that were featured in the World of Poetry.

Budget Book

January 1st, 1947 to September 15th, 1947

When Angelo returned from serving on a weather station in Canada with The United States Army Air Force during World War 2, he and Genevieve married and built a house on Angelo's family farm at the South West intersection of Christmas Tree Road and RR1 (Now called Herrin Rd.) in rural Williamson County. Her father, Freeman Pate, was a carpenter and used the wood reclaimed from a store they tore down in Herrin, IL to frame out the house. According to a notebook, titled the Budget Book, they borrowed $390.00 ($5,564 in 2024 dollars) from his parents, Paul and Delena Merlo to help build the house. They paid off the money they borrowed on September 15th, 1947.

Paul and his wife, Angelo's parents, emigrated from Northern Italy to North America and bought a 20 acre farm with an old farm house from the Bandy family. Paul Merlo worked as a coal miner, Delena was a homemaker. They raised their four children,

Celeste, Virginia, Rose, and Angelo on the farm.

The following entries are from a homemade weekly ledger, titled 'Budget Book' kept by Genevieve of monies paid and earned while they were building their house in 1947. Amounts are in U.S. Dollars (USD).

Wages varied from $43.00 to $58.00 per week

ITEM / COST

2-Baby Dresses $1.26
Maternity Gown 50¢
Flashlight $1.30
Gasoline $2.00
Shelf $1.50
Cough Medicine and Books 65¢
Medicine, Vicks, and Shampoo 39¢
Watch Cleaning and Sears $5.00
Stove $75.00
Corner Cabinet $21.00
Insurance $12.00
Doctor $10.00
Shades $1.48
Hat $1.52
Haircut 75¢
Payment to Teamsters Union $4.00
Eggs 82¢
Oil 55¢
Curtain $2.50
Cigarettes 68¢

Ice Cream 25¢
Steak 75¢
Purse $2.50
Pipe for Sink $1.50
Radio $22.00
Car Repair $12.00
Lunch 50¢
200lb Chicken Feed $9.50
Recreation $5.06
Dentist $4.00
Sewing Machine $16.00
Angelo's Shoes Fixed $1.55
Window Spray and Candy 50¢
Pigs and Wheat $17.00
Food (Weekly Groceries) $10.00
Broom $1.39
100 Chickens $16.50
Gas for Stove $9.20
Donation 50¢
New Washing Machine $123.00
Shirt $2.00
Neck Tie $1.00
Hospital $32.20
Meat and Bread $1.00
Piggy Bank 70¢
Hair Do $5.00
Electric Iron $5.00

Some of the entries were recurring payments, most are actual cost of the items or expenditures. More money was borrowed and paid back to the parents in 1948, but the records were not complete. In the late 1970's Angelo and Genevieve bought the farm outright from Angelo's sisters.

World of Poetry Award 1

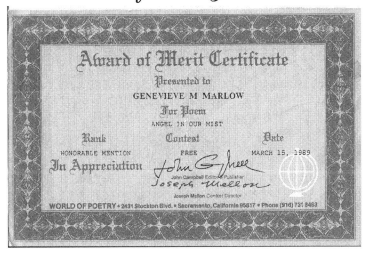

World of Poetry Award 2

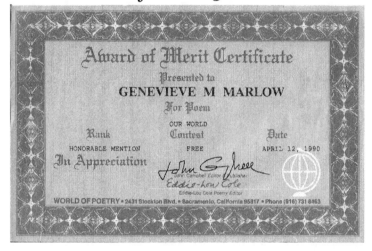

Sacrifice of a Mother

What does it Mean, Being a Mother?
It is Not being able to Give Birth
But Giving Up Your Freedom for Another
A Baby, The Most Important Thing on Earth

Getting Up Nights at the First Cry
Of a Baby, Who is Fretful or a Child
Baking Cookies when You Prefer Pie
Just to See that Sweet Little Smile

Doing without Extra Clothes or Treat
Giving Up a Longed for Vacation
Scrimping for Vitamins, and Fruit to Eat
Thanking God for Each Perfect Creation

Mothers, Some Women it is Only an Illusion
In the Paper Everyday We do Read
Children Tortured, the Only One Conclusion
Some Women, Children They Don't Need

I'm Thankful, We only had Three
Although I'm Very Proud of Them
Of the Responsibility, Now I am Free
Free, to Come and Go on a Whim

How Thankful We All Should Be

Housework Today I cannot Concentrate
For it is Raining Dark and Gray
Too Many Jobs to Numerate
But I'm afraid I'm too Late Today

How Thankful We All Should Be
To be Able to See this Lovely Fall
I Hope in the Heavens I will Be
For I can Look Down and See it All

The People on Earth I could Ignore
I would only See the Beautiful Places
The Beauty in My Heart I could Store
And Not See the Tortured Sad Faces

I could See the Geese as they Fly By
In Harmony and Perfect Formation
So Lovely against the Blue of the Sky
One More Thing that is of God's Creation

To See the Birds, all Colors and Hues
Flying from Tree to Tree

All Colors, Brown, Gray, Red, and Blue
There are still a Few that are Free

Only the Young Children are Happy and Care Free
With No Worries, Troubles, or Woes
Some are Hungry and that should Not Be
For Many have a Rough Road to Hoe

I Do Not Believe this World will Change
There will be More Sin and Corruption
More People Murdered and Deranged
Until the World has one Big Eruption

Then God will come Down and Pick up the Pieces
To Judge and Reward His Very Own
The Book of Life, Our Greatest Thesis
But Then it will be Too Late to Cry and Moan

Every One Alive has Some Regret
Something in the Past or Left Undone
Not to Man but to God should We Fret
Because We've let Down His Only Son

A Loved One You Can Hold

Lord, I Thank Thee for thy Love
The Sky, Clouds, and Stars Above
Rain, Sleet, and the Snow
And Ability to Watch the Streams Flow

For the many Friends, and Neighbors Too
You Gave each of Us so very Much
Though We don't Act it, We do Love You
Although in Trouble, You are Our Crutch

Without You what would We Do?
I Pray that All will Praise Thy Name
We Call and Pray When Ill or Blue
And to get to Heaven is Our Aim

As We open Our Eyes each Day
Or Whatever Time it may Be
The Very First Words We should Say
Is Thank You God, We Love Thee

We are Free to Love and to Live
Any way that We may Desire
Whatever We do, God does Forgive
And His Love for Us will never Tire

We Should Thank Him for the very Air
And the Job, Whatever it might Be
Our Troubles He is willing to Share
And Our Future whatever He may See

Visit a Hospital or Nursing Home
Then Your Blessings will seem Twofold
Thank God for Two Legs on which to Roam
Or a Loved One that You can Hold

Thank Him for the Sun and the Rain
For without Both, We would be Lost
Thank Him, for each Joy and Pain
Remember how He Died, on the Cross

Blue Pigeon

A Small Blue Pigeon was Found
Ang. Found him Helpless Near the Barn
Cold and Fluttering on the Ground
Afraid the Dogs would do him Harm

We took Care of him All Winter Long
For at first he Could Not use his Wing
A very weak Coo was his only Song
As We waited for the Coming Spring

The Cage, he didn't Care for at First
And Would Sit in a corner with his Head Down
Soon he began to Hunger and Thirst
So We put him Gently on the Ground

Every Day We opened the Door
And waited for him to Fly Out
But he was Still Weak and Poor
And could Hardly get About

One Day he decided to Try his Wings
And was Gone for a Couple of Days
Another Pigeon at home he Brings
Home for a Little While he Stays

One Night he went into the Chicken House
Where he was Contented or so We Thought
For they were as Quiet as a Mouse
A Place for their Little Nest they Sought

So Now there is a Little Nest
And Two Little Eggs are in It
The Little Mate went back to Rest
As Our Pigeon on the Nest does Sit

One Family One Earth

This Beautiful World of Ours
That Our Lord gave Us for a While
The Rivers, Trees, Wildlife, and Flowers
Sunrise and a Baby's Smile

As We Open Our Eyes at Birth
And See Our Loved Ones Near
Such Beauty abounds on Our Earth
Destroying It is Our Greatest Fear

How many Years will it Take
For Our Animals, Fowl, and Fish to Die?
The Trees, Grass, and Gardens Bake
Recycle, Every Family has to Try

Man has One Family, One Earth
To Protect from Toxic Waste and Pollution
The Animals and Birds We Protect from Birth
Cleaning Up Our Planet is the Only Solution

Pick up Cans along the Highway
And Paper and Glass on the Street
Aluminum You can Sell for Pay
If We Don't try We are Bound for Defeat

We Continue to Hear about Global Warming
Animal and Plant Resources We Ignore
Not Realizing how many People We are Harming
Not Tomorrow but Now at Our Door

Binitos

If You haven't been to Binitos
Then You have Missed a Rare Treat
They have Pizza, Italian Beef, and Tacos
Just a Few of the Foods They have to Eat

They have Barbecue and Hamburgers with Cheese
Also French Fries and the Best Onion Rings
Even Ice Cream any kind You Please
Come Over and Some Hungry Friends Do Bring

They also have Hamburgers of Any Size
With Lots of Good Lean Meat
Try Them, You are in for a Surprise
And Their Prices can't be Beat

Their Service is Really First Rate
And They have Plenty of Parking Space
The Owner is the Very Nice, Earl A. Pate
You'll not See Him, which is Usually the Case

Why Not Try Their Special Today?
One Dollar gets Hamburger, Fries, and Coke
And that's Little Enough to Pay
So No One goes Home Unhappy or Broke

(July 4th, 1976)

When I Was Young

When I was Young and Full of Dreams
Of Foreign Places and Sights to See
Old Age wasn't in My Scheme
For it would Never happen to Me

I Thought Thirty was Oh So Old
And Grey Hair, Oh No, not for Me
You'll get Old, I was Told
No, I'll Die Young You will See

But Now I am Fifty Two
You Know that Seems Almost Young
The Years Ahead may be Few
But for Now, Life has Just Begun

Christmas 1972

Christmas is almost Here
The Home with Beauty Shines
Such a Lovely Time of Year
Trees of All Shapes and Kinds

The Bustle of the Streets and Stores
Children with Sweet Shining Faces
Singing Modern and Folklore
Dolls of many Countries and Races

How We Honor that Little Babe
Who's Birthday We Celebrate
Can Our Debt ever Be Paid?
To Him whose Birthday We Anticipate

God Forgive Us, Lest We Forget
The Meaning of This Day
There is Sorrow and Trouble I Regret
May All of It End, I Pray

Soon Christmas will be Gone
As will Some of the Love and Kindness to All
Nothing Ahead but Days Cold and Long
Lights and Trees put away until Next Fall

GENEVIEVE MAE MARLOW

Now, We shall Start a New Year
With Our Good Wishes and Resolutions
Some will Celebrate with Wine and Beer
Which will play Havoc with Their Constitution

What Lies Ahead Who but God Alone Knows
And May Love Among Mankind Grow

Hopeless Situation

Our Blessed Lord His Son did Send
To Save the World and All of Mankind
His Flock He was to Seek and to Tend
If any of His Sheep He could Find

Divorce, Sin, and Corruption have Spread
And Little Children have had to Pay
The Devil has Taken Over Instead
For Not Enough of Us have begun to Pray

Disease and Poverty among the Population
Even the Weather, it has Gone Wild
Man is in a Hopeless Situation
For His Sins in Heaven have been Filed

We Keep Thinking it can Get No Worse
But We are Closing Our Eyes I Fear
For We are only Beginning a Worse Curse
Until the Day Our Lord Does Appear

Michelle

November 30

Today is the 30th of November
A Year ago Today, the Day was Sad
A Day that We will Always Remember
Michelle was Take to St. Louis Very Bad

To Look at Her Now, You wouldn't Believe It
Such a Pretty and Healthy Child
To Heal Her, Our Lord did see Fit
Now Other Problems on Her has Piled

She Walks Oh So Very Well
And Has Ten Teeth So Far
You Fall but Do Not Yell
And Love Riding in a Car

Aunt Jeek got You a Red Dress
In it You Look Like a Doll
Went to Church and I Must Confess
I won't Take You again for a While

You Talked All of the Way Through
Though No One Knew what You Said
Everyone had Their Eyes on You
A Pretty Little Doll in a Dress of Red

Sleep My Baby the Whole Night Through
For You have Played so Hard all Day
May Our Lord continue to Watch Over You
And Guide Your Every Step All the Way

How Precious You Look when You Sleep
Those Little Arms spread Wide
Are Your Dreams Light or Deep?
As You clutch Your Doll by Your Side

About Two O' Clock You Still Wake Up
For Your Bottle of Warm Milk
At Times You only Take a Sup
So Sleepy the Bottle You Cannot Tilt

Beans in the Field

Our Luck continues to Amaze Me
The Ground is Just drying Out
Combining our Beans is Not to Be
It's Raining Again on Our Route

The Clouds are like dirty Snow Banks
As they drift Slowly across the Moon
The Weatherman's Prediction Really Stinks
Most of our Beans are Surely Doomed

If just Once We could get a Break
But for Us that will Never Be
The Fields are more Like a Lake
It is a Terrible Thing to See

November 20th and Beans Still in the Field
Rained again and No One can Combine
We Would have had a Very Good Yield
But there is No Hope of getting them Out on Time

They were Going to Combine Tomorrow
But, as usual, it Rained Again Tonight
All kinds of Combines to Borrow
Now the Beans are Rotten and look Afright

25th of November, and the ground's Finally Dry
So on the Phone to get Someone to Combine
One Man said He would come Over and Try
Our 6 inches of Snow came, at the Very Worst Time

Thanksgiving is Past, and Christmas draws Near
But only a Few Farmers can Rejoice
The Rains have brought a whole New Fear
In Our Weather We do not have a Choice

I Do believe the Rush began Today
For Christmas Shoppers were all Over
A Few People must have Spent their Whole Pay
With Mines Striking it Won't be a Bed of Clover

The Weather has Turned for the Worst
In the Teens and with Wind Chills Below Zero
With Unstable Weather We have been Cursed
And They Predict a Couple of Days in a Row

A Poem About Spring

Today is Lovely, this First Day of May
Everything is Green although still Cool
We Know that it Will Not stay this Way
We'll Jump into Summer is the usual Rule

Spring is Here there is No Doubt
So Summer can't be Far Away
All of the Flowers are Beginning to Sprout
As the Green Leaves in the Wind Sway

Lots of Wind and Too Much Rain
Too Wet to Work in the Field
Lots of Flu with Aches and Pain
Men getting out their Rods and Reels

How Lovely the Sky on a Spring Night
Even the Stars seem to have an Extra Glow
In the North, the Lightning So Bright
As it Darts about To and Fro

At Last now We can Turn the Heat Off
At Last Summer seems to be Here
Cold's still Here and People still Cough
Now no more Bad Weather do We Fear

We are now in the Midst of Our Growing Season
When even a Sprinkle means Money or Loss
One Day it is Hot the Next Day is Freezing
But the Farmers still Plant No Matter the Cost

Look Outside, what do You See?
What Beauty on Us the Lord has Bestowed
Flowers Everywhere, the Green of the Trees
But Our Own Destiny We cannot Control

The Wind is Blowing, a Storm is Brewing
Trees are Bending, the Sky is without Light
Limbs Falling in the Yard Strewing
Every Creature Scurrying to get Out of Sight

The Seasons

Winter, Spring, Summer and Fall
Each of the Seasons have a Special Allure
There is Something to Love in them All
And All of them We have to Endure

Winter has a Lot of Headaches
With its Colds, Sore Throats and Flu
We're always Glad to See it Break
For Our Pretty Days have been Few

Spring, I guess is the Best of them All
As the Land gets Ready for a New Birth
With Everything Dying in the Fall
New Life Begins from the Good Earth

Summer is a Great Season for Some
If They can Afford to Stay at the Lake
With Air Condition it is More Fun
But a Lot of Electricity it does Take

Fall, with its Lovely Colors Around
But all Too soon it Too is Gone
Dead Leaves and Bareness Abound
It doesn't Stay around Very Long

ANGEL'S REFLECTION

But Wouldn't it be Awfully Dull
If Our Temp. was Always the Same
The Bad from the Good We could Cull
And the Winds and Rain could Tame

I Pray that We can Overcome, the Obstacles of Life
To Accept with Patience and No Remorse
Problems that can't be Solved with Money or Knife
But have to be Taken with a Matter of Course

To Accept God's Will in All that Matters
Even unto Illness or Even unto Death
Life has Many a Rung on the Ladder
So Many before We go to a Final Rest

My Dearest Husband

My Dearest Husband, May I Wish You Well
On This, Our Very, Very Special Day
I Don't Remember the Hour or Why I Fell
In Love with You, but I will Never Sway

You have been the Better Part of Me
And These 25 years have been the Best
We've had Trouble, and Sorrow We may See
But Together We can Stand the Test

My Days Began when You get Home
My Thoughts are Always of You
I'm Most Contented when We're Alone
No Matter My Husband, What We Do

Some Wonder Why We stay Home
But Happiness is Being Together
There are People who have to Roam
Regardless of the Time or Weather

Death Will part Us, and bring Us Strife
But I Pray it is Years and Years from Now
It has been a Pleasure just Being Your Wife
And to God's Will We shall Always Bow

Father

Father, What Does the Word Mean?
One Who Works Hard Every Day
For many hours He is Never Seen
Always Thankful for a Full Week's Pay

The Same old Grind Day or Night
Just Barely eking out a Living
At times Worried and Uptight
Always Loving and Forgiving

Knowing there are So Many Work years Ahead
Trying to Pay Bills and Save Money
Always there is Worry and the Dread
That Someone will come Running

Providing His Family with the Good Things of Life
Never asking for Nothing in Return
Too Proud to Cry in times of Strife
From Him so much We Could Learn

Some Men and Fathers Never Grow Up
And Their Families suffer the Consequence
From Responsibilities They Drank or Sup
As We surely Know from the Evidence

A Valentine to My Husband

A Special Note to a Very Dear Friend
Who just happens to Be my Husband Too
One Day Our Life on Earth will come to an End
And Our Years together have been too Few

For Another Man I've Never Cared
As I've always Cared for You
I've Enjoyed the Years We've Shared
Without You I wouldn't know What to Do

The Days are so Very Long
Waiting for You to Come Home
It isn't the Same when You are Gone
Even Though I don't Mind being Alone

I've had Everything I've Ever Wished For
Since You asked Me to Be Your Wife
How Nice it will be when You Retire
And We can Really begin Our Life

Now that Our Sons are Married and Gone
We can Begin our Second Honeymoon
I Pray Our years together will Be Long
That God will not Separate Us too Soon

For that is the Only Way I will ever Part
For You my Husband have been my Life
You have Always and Forever had my Heart
I Thank You for Making Me your Wife

Happy Valentine to My Husband
Who has my Heart throughout the Year
You are always There to Hold my Hand
When I'm Ill or when in Fear

Cards and Candy are Very Nice
But I Know I'm Loved without Them
Through Fair Weather, Snow, and Ice
My Husband knows that I Love Him

I Know that One Day We will Part
Our Lord has Told Us So
But, Ang, You Know You have My Heart
That I Love You, of Course you Know

Your Loving Wife.

To My Husband

February 14, 1971

Honey, Today is Valentine's Day
And I Love You with all My Heart
Always with Me in Work or Play
Not Many Times have We been Apart

To just come Out and Say to Your Face
I Love You, is Hard for Me to Do
So Writing This has its Place
For I Really and Truly do Love You

I Know that I've Loved only One Man
Some may Love Quite a Few
No One may Hold My Hand
For There's No One but You

I've Loved You since First We Met
Oh how the Months and Years did Fly
The Times We Missed is My One Regret
But, I'll Love You until I Die

To Buy a Card would be the Easy Way
But I Thought I would Save You Money
Since it would Come out of Your Pay
And That wouldn't be So Funny

May I Live Each Day

May I Live Each Day as if I'll Die any Minute
And Not even Think of Tomorrow
I'll Enjoy this World and What's in It
Not Thinking of the Past and its Sorrow

Of Course Mistakes I have Made
So I Shall Try to do a Lot Better
And Finish the Plans I have Laid
Especially Catching up on Writing Letters

Perhaps I'll not Be Here to do These Things
So Now You will Know I Planned To
I'll Print My ideas and Put them in Frames
I don't Know, for I have Quite a Few

Wouldn't Most of Us Panic if We knew what's Ahead
Because Life has a way of Changing
Just Be Thankful You're Walking and Not in Bed
You can See and Hear the Birds Singing

Some People are a Lot Worse Off than We
And There are Some Who may be Crying Inside
Oh how Happy and Grateful We should Be
That in America We do Abide

Over Forty

Life Begins at Forty, so They Say
For Old Age with its Aches, I Do Agree
The Offspring have Gone their Way
And Without Glasses You cannot See

To Hear, You have to Read Lips
And Arthritis, it seems to Take Over
Coffee and Tea you only take One Sip
If more then, Sleep is no Bed of Clover

Grandchildren are Sweet but get on Your Nerves
And You get Upset at the Least Little Thing
Yes, Old Age sometimes, it Throws you a Curve
Just a Few things that Old Age will Bring

Grandchildren come to Visit, and You don't Mind
But You're Responsible when They get Hurt
You're too Obliging and Sometimes too Kind
When at times You should be a Little Curt

For the Most Part Old Age is Alright
At Least you can Get a Good Night's Rest
And Don't Stay Awake half of the Night
Waiting for Kids that put You Through Life's Test

People without Children don't Know about Trouble
From the Time They are Born Worry sets In
The House is always Filled with Rubble
To Scold, Dr. Spock says is a Sin

If I had a Chance to Do it Over
Would I have had My Three Boys?
But Life is Never a Bed of Clover
And They have Brought Tears and Joy

Grandchildren, now We have Four
And One More on the Way
So We are Rich Though We are Poor
And What More is there to Say?

No Stars at Night

The Moon Looks so Weird Tonight
As the Clouds Cast over it a Haze
How Dark it is Without the Light
No Twinkling of the Stars on which to Gaze

Just to have Sight and Count the Stars
The Great Galaxy up so Very High
To Dream of Things from Afar
To See the Airplanes as They go By

Let Others Live Life as they Please
Don't Interpret the Bible as You Wish
Their's Different, Don't give Them the Freeze
Not Everyone Likes the Same Dish

It Seems like Most Bad Things
Happen in the Dead of Night
Even Now when the Telephone Rings
My Heart Skips a Beat with Fright

But Still there is Such Beauty
On a Quiet Warm Summer Night
As Night Life goes about its Duties
Waiting for the First Ray of Day Light

One Long Curse

Parenthood, where is All of the Glory
That We've Read about Throughout the Ages
If We only Knew the True to Life Story
Or what is Hid Behind the Pages

Sure there was a Few Pleasant Days
A Few through the Years as I Remember
When the Boys were Healthy and at Play
Or the First Day of School in September

There was Always Something to Worry About
Either No Money or One of Them was Ill
A Broken Window, a Quarrel or Shout
By Night My Voice had become Pretty Shrill

I Thought it couldn't Possibly get any Worse
But Boy I was in for a Rude Surprise
I Could have used a Good Psychiatrist Nurse
Especially when that 16th Birthday Arrived

Then They started Dating and going Around
And I worried until I Heard their Car
I think All Parents should be Heaven Bound
From Insanity They aren't Very Far

So They get Married and You Hope for the Best
Don't get Excited for that is Only an Illusion
Now You think You will get a Little Rest
It's Hopeless, is the Only Conclusion

Their Troubles usually are brought Back Home
And You Still can't Relax and Enjoy Life
No, They don't Run Around or Roam
Now You have their Worries and their Wife's

We Wonder what the Future will Be
Will it be Better or Worse?
From Worry will We ever be Free?
Or is Life just One Long Curse?

God's Eyes

This Morning it is The 4th of May
The Year of 19 and 72
The Sky is Cloudy and Gray
The Flowers and Trees are Minus their Dew

Spring is Here and the Grass is Turning Green
And the Trees are in All of their Glory
The Most Beautiful Sight to be Seen
Only God could Produce such a Story

Summer, it will Soon be Here
And We'll all be Trying to Keep Cool
Oh it Will be Hot, do Not Fear
But We can always go Sit in the Pool

When We're Cold, We Wish it was Warm
Why Can't We be Happy, What ever is to Be
If We have Cover to get Out of the Storm
And Blessed with Sight, so the Beauty We See

Each Day we Live Should be as Our Last
For We do Not Know about Tomorrow
Just Look Back and See how Fast
The Years have Passed on Happiness and Sorrow

So We Thank You God for Each Day
For Our Health and the Health of Others
Protect Us in Work and Play
And May We, All Love God and Our Brothers

Our Life on Earth is Like a Flower
We could be Gone any Minute or Hour

That Our Heart will Fail to Beat
And Turn Cold, with No More Heat

Will We go Out like a Clock?
With just One More Tick and then will Stop

Or Linger on until We are No More
And God has Opened the Mighty Door

Then We shall See the Beauty and Grace
Of Heaven and God's Beautiful Face

I have Seen God's Mother in a Dream
It was the Most Lovely Face I've Ever Seen

One Time I Saw Only God's Eyes
The Blessing I received made Me Survive
Because I was Ill and He came to Me
Only His Beautiful Eyes He Let Me See
The Compassion and Love I Cannot Describe
Not Drawings nor Poems, could I Decide
I can Still See Him and Oh! what a Sight
He Came and Blessed Me one Lonely Night

Timmy Lee

Today I Visited My First Angel
The Love that Shines from His Eyes
With Crowds of People He does not Mingle
How He has Enriched So Many Lives

His Name is None Other than Timmy Lee
Who Never Meets an Enemy or a Stranger
He Loves Everyone that He Sees
And Knows of No Fear or of Danger

His Greatest Joy is to Give to Others
If Only a Small Piece of Candy
Everyone He Meets is His Brother
And His Favorite Toy is a Little Panda

There are So Many People on this Earth
Who Swear They are Headed for the Pearly Gates
But Timmy has been Saved a Special Birth
For Many Others, It will be Too Late

He Can't Marry or Run Around
But Neither did Jesus, as You Recall
He was also Heavenly Bound
Of Sin, Timmy will Never Fall

In Heaven He will have a Special Place
That God has Already for Him in Store
Don't Feel Sad when Looking at that Sweet Face
But for God! Do just a Little Bit More

At Times His Parents do Ponder
Why did this Happen to Me?
But They Doubt No More or could be Fonder
Of Their Special Angel, Timmy Lee

Do Not ever Covet or Envy Others
For Some have Every Blessing on this Earth
Do They Treat Everyone as Their Brother?
Has God Saved for Them a Special Birth?

God did Not Promise Happiness on Earth
But Only in Heaven would Our Paradise Be
If Only We Prove to Him Our Actual Worth
How Lucky He Gave Us Our Timmy Lee

Do not Pity the Timmy's of this Earth
For They are so Much More Fortunate than We
God already Knows of Timmy's Worth
He's Paid His Price and of Heaven He Will See

Thorns in Our Crown

Life is Like a Swing or an Elevator
As it seems to Always be Up or Down
One Day We'll Return to Our Creator
Will there be Gold or Thorns in Our Crown?

Will We be Remembered for Very Long?
Will Our Friends and Loved Ones Forget?
Have We Did Anyone any Wrong?
Did We ask Forgiveness or Regret?

Is Our House Clean and in Order?
With Our Lord and All Mankind
Were We Always just on the Border?
Were We First or at the End of the Line?

Our World has So Much Love and Beauty
But it Seems to be Filled with Deceit
Do We go to Church just Out of Duty
Or to Make Our Lives More Complete?

One Day We will Not Wake Up
From Our Nightmare, or was it a Dream?
God will Not Offer Us Another Cup
No matter How Religious We do Seem

This World is Only a Stopping Place
For the Long Journey that is Ahead
I Pray that I will be Filled with Grace
The Moment before I'm Pronounced Dead

What a Great Mystery Death Must Be
Or Our Lord would Not have Died
He Did Not have to Die for You or Me
But to Wash Away Our Sins, He Surely Tried

Sickness and Worry, Torture and Death
That, We can All Expect Sooner or Later
So with Our Remaining Voice and Breath
Ask Forgiveness and Love for Our Creator

When Life Seems Hopeless and We have No Hope
Instead of Smiling You Want to Cry
You Think You are at the End of Your Rope
Don't give Up, for Your Lord is Standing By

As I Lay Sleepless

As I lay Sleepless and Restless in Bed
Thinking of Present and of the Past
Perhaps I would be Better Off Dead
Then the Last Stone would be Cast

I was Born under an Unlucky Star
For Few Pleasures I have Had
My Life has been Useless So Far
And Most of it has been Sad

I have a Pretty Nice Home
And Three Very Fine Boys
A Husband who doesn't Roam
But Still Very few Joys

What is the Meaning of Love?
It has to be More than This
You can't Hurt and Shove
And Wipe it away with a Kiss

You Cannot Hurt and Belittle a Wife
In Front of People, Slander and Disgrace
That isn't Very Much of a Life
When You continue to Lose Face

If Only when Young, We had the Maturity
To Figure and try to Look Ahead
Not Settle for False Security
But Think Things out Instead

But, When Young and Home is Hell
You're just Looking for a Way Out
It's Much Worse than One can Tell
You're Ashamed to Say what it's all About

So You go Looking for Something Better
Anything to get Out of this Mess
From an Aunt you get a Letter
What You're leaving it Can't be Much Less

So You Hope for a Better Life
Something that Promises More
But all you get is More Heartache and Strife
So again on Happiness you Close the Door

After a Few Years You again Smile
For Your First and Only Love is Home
If only Time We could Turn Back Awhile
And for Lost Time not to Moan

I have Not had Heaven on Earth
And inner Happiness I have Not Seen
So I Pray for an Upper Birth
God and I Know I haven't been That Mean

This Is My House

This is My House and I am the Queen
Though Nothing Fancy, This is My Throne
Sometimes it doesn't Look Extra Clean
I Love it, because it is My Home

No Other Place had I Rather Be
For this is Where I am Content
Foreign Places do not Interest Me
This is Mine and I don't Pay Rent

Christmas is Drawing Near
And People are Full of Joy
Soon it will be a Brand New Year
Children are Dreaming of Toys

For Some there is Sadness and Tears
And Christmas makes it All the Worse
Pray that God will also Bring Them Cheer
Nothing Helps, Not even a Filled Purse

Perhaps at Times I am Kind of Sassy
And My Manners not up to Par
Only in My Home am I Happy
For in My Home I am the Star

GENEVIEVE MAE MARLOW

I would Like to have a Fancy House
But there is Things that Mean Much More
I don't care for Beethoven or Strauss
Sure I would Rather be Rich than Poor

But Over this I won't Lose any Sleep
For Tomorrow I may not Be Here
It's not too Fancy but Mine to Keep
And Who Knows about Next Year

Happy Father's Day

    F - Is for the Faith You've Shown these Many Years
    A - Is for the Attention Through the Good and Bad
    T - Is for all of the Tomorrows Through Happiness and Tears
    H - Is for Happiness and Sadness that We've Had
    E - Is for the Energy to Put Up with Me
    R - Is for the Respect that in Your Eyes I See

My Dearest Husband I could use All of the Alphabet
And Still not Say All that I Feel
Though There are Times I Fuss and Fret
It is Hard to Realize, that You are Real

I Would Not Trade You for Any Price
Even Though There are Days when I'm Blue
Why Would I have Married You Twice
Because Men Like You are Very Few

Almost any Man can Father a Child
But it takes Someone Special to be a Dad
Coming Home Tired and Still Trying to Smile

When One of the Boys has been Unruly or Bad

Helping with School Work when Feeling Low
Replacing a Broken Window with
No Money to Spare
Keeping Our Spirits Up when Life
had Dealt a Hard Blow
Knowing that in the Many Ways You Show You Care

Working Long Hours both Night and Day
Asking Nothing for Yourself but a Glass of Beer
Putting Up with all Kinds of Hardships for Little Pay
Trying not to Show Your Doubts and Fears

Yes Any Man can be a Father
But How Many Really Act like One?
Most Men would Think it Too Much Bother
To Stay Home at Night and Help with Three Sons

So, Happy Father's Day to a Very Special Dad
I'm Proud He is the Father to Our Three Boys
There are Many Parents that are Very Sad
For Their Children haven't brought Them Joy

Thank God that Our Sons are Grown
And of Them We are Proud
A Good Example You have Shown
For They would Stand Out in Any Crowd

I'm Very Much a Liberated Wife
For Here is Where I Love to Be
My Home and Family are My Life
So Thank You to My Husband for Loving Me

Happy Father's Day,
With Love,
Your Wife

Waiting is Never Over

From the Time of Birth, it Seems We Wait
Waiting to be Born, then Waiting to be Fed
Crying if the Feeding is a Little Bit Late
Taking Our First Step and Waiting to be Led

As a Child We Wait for Christmas, Easter or Birthday
The New Clothes, Presents, Candy and Toys
No Worries about Anything Except the Delay
And the Promise of Being Good Girls and Boys

All Too Soon We are in School
And Waiting to See Your Report Card
If Bad, Feeling like a Dummy or a Fool
If the Lessons for You are a Little Too Hard

Then that Important Day, You Reach Your Teens
It is Your First Dance or Your First Date
The Hour's So Slow, like Days or So it Seems
Walking the Floor if He is Just a Little Late

Then the Greatest Moment in Your Life Arrives
That Special Boy asks for Your Hand in Marriage
You don't Know How You'll Ever Survive
Until You have a Baby in that Perfect Carriage

You Wait through all Kinds of Baby Ills
The First Step, First Tooth and First Smile
Of Sleepless Nights You've had Your Fill
And Dream of Vacation and Getting
Away for a While

You Worry and Wonder What's Ahead
They Reach Sixteen and the Driver's Test
They take Out the Car, You Wait and Dread
And Pray They'll be Home Soon so You can Rest

One Day They Too get Married and Leave Home
With a Sigh You Think the Waiting is Over
The Last One is Gone and You're Finally Alone
But You're still Looking for that Four Leaf Clover

Then You are Waiting for that First Grandchild
Will it be a Boy or Girl and be Alright
You Think the Waiting will Drive You Wild
Still Frightened when the Phone Rings at Night

Waiting is Never Over until Your Death
Then No More Waiting for the Phone to Ring
What Day or Hour will You Breathe Your Last Breath
And what Blessings will it Bring?

Fall

The Fall Season has Begun
And Halloween is almost Here
Children playing Tricks and having Fun
In Windows, Smiling Pumpkins Appear

The Fall Air is Brisk and Cold
Some Windows are Already Soaped
Trick and Treaters are getting Bold
But Parents are Trying to Cope

How Lovely the Trees, Red, Orange, and Yellow
Like a Beautiful Painting of Old
The Drought has left Ponds and Creeks Shallow
As Our Winter Season begins to Unfold

The Coal and Logs Laid up for the Winter
And Our Coats still Smell of Moth Balls
As We Prepare for Our Thanksgiving Dinner
And Wait for the Very First Snow Fall

A Few Christmas Presents have been Laid Aside
And I Never Cease to Feel the Anticipation
Although we Take God's Work in Stride
I'm Glad to Live in this Generation

Travel

The Rain Outside, so Lovely and Quiet
Gently falling on a Thirsty Earth
Like Diamonds the Rain Drops in the Light
The Grain in the Fields given a New Birth

What a Blessing it Truly Must Be
To Be able to Draw God's Wondrous Sights
The Beauty all around We See
Wherever We Look out Day or Night

I Would Love to Travel Far and Wide
To See a Mountain and Foreign Places
Just to be Able to See an Ocean Tide
Or See the Beauty of all the Races

But there is Not Another Place like Home
Because that is Where My Heart will Be
Sure I would like to See Paris or Rome
But in the United States, There I Know I'm Free

What if

If Every Day You would Know in Advance
How Exactly Tomorrow would Be
No Rain or Sleet on the Roof would Dance
Or if We had to Pay for the Beauty We See

If there Never was Any Sadness or Joy
No Illness, no Sun, or any Wind or Moon
No Children to Love, Resent or Annoy
If to Life We had to Dance a Different Tune

No God on which We could Lean
To Turn to when Life gets Rough
Have a Forgiving Heart, never Mean
To have Everything but Never Enough

If Winter was Constant, Cold, and Dreary
No Sun and Trees Bare and Forlorn
Instead of Breaks with the Sun so Cheery
With Birds Singing in the Early Morn

If Everyday was Always the Same
How Dull Our Life would Be
And Our Summers Mild and Tame
And No Grass or Leaves on the Trees

If Everyday You would Know in Advance
How Exactly Tomorrow would Be

Over the Hill Gang

The Senior Citizens at their Best
You'd Think Bowling was their Life
Never taking Time Out for a Rest
Trying to Forget their Aches and Strife

Bowling is a Whole Lot of Fun
Each Team trying their Best to Win
But When the Day is Done
You've Laughed and Made a New Friend

Bowling is a Most Aggravating Game
A Strike and the Next a Gutter Ball
Although We'll Never get Fame
It's such a Joy to see the Pins Fall

In Baseball, Three Strikes You're Out
In Bowling they Flash a Turkey
Instead of Boos You Hear a Shout
And Walking Back Pretty Perky

Yes, the Senior Citizens are on a Roll
And Bowling is Our Favorite Game
Just Stop and Visit the S.I. Bowl
In Lights You'll See Our Name

Bowling

Bowling will drive You to Drink
And I don't Mean Water
It can drive You Over the Brink
Or make You feel Like Mortar

You Stand just where They Say
And hold the Ball just So
But then it will Go the Wrong Way
Or in the Gutter it will Go

Then You'll get Three Strikes Straight
Or maybe Knock Down Two
At times Miss the Other Eight
And with Luck, get a Few

Keep Your arm Straight and Thumb Up
The Second Arrow is where You Aim
Glance at the Score and an Empty Cup
Bowling, It's just an Impossible Game

A Good Sport to keep You in Shape
Bowling or just Visiting with a Friend
The Bloopers I'd like to have On Tape
Winning, on That, You just Can't Depend

The Sweet Hearts

Bowling, the Game of Fear
You Never Know where the Ball will Go
Always a Pin Hiding in the Rear
And to Get it, It takes a Pro

And One Set that is a Nightmare
Is the Seven and the Ten Pin
That Split is a Scary Pair
Missing One, on that you can Depend

Our Team is now The Sweet Hearts
There is Wanda, Evelyn, Jenny, and Penny
At Times We're All out of Sorts
And Strikes We don't get Any

But We still Try and have a Ball
For We've met a lot of New Friends
Encouraging One another as the Pins Fall
And doing some New Knee Bends

The Devil Has Been Loosed

Life is what We Make of It
Mistakes, All of Us have Made
In Heaven, a Candle has been Lit
Of the Future We Need not be Afraid

The Stars in Heaven Shall Light Our Way
As We Climb the Stairs to Glory
Asking for Forgiveness as We Pray
Reading Our Bible for God's Own Story

We Know Not what Lies in Store
For the Future what Does it Hold
Will it be Exciting or a Bore?
What is the Mystery yet Untold?

Trouble and Strife Throughout the Globe
Hunger, Illness and Death
No Different when Man divided Our Lord's Robe
Taunting and Cursing Him until His Last Breath

Divorce, and Death to the Innocent
The Devil has been Loosed from His Chains
We Pray to Our Lord and Cry in Lament
But Satan Seems to have Full Reign

Death, the Last Chance for Happiness and Peace
For on Earth, It is not To Be
A Few Years God has let us Lease
A Glimpse of Heaven, He will Not let Us See

I Do Not Fear Death or the Here After
It is Why We were all Born
No more Illness and Hate, only Laughter
With Joy We go to Our Higher Dome

We Say, We are not Afraid to Die
But Everyone Hates to Pack and Leave
No One has Come Back to Tell Us Why
Or what We will See or Receive

Here for a Little While

As I Lay in My Last Bed
They Say that I am Dead

But, I Know I'm only Asleep
For God Came and Took Me to Keep

I was Here for a Little While
So Dry Your Eyes and Try to Smile

Please Don't Rant and Rave
And Ruin the Beauty of This Day

We Knew that This Day would Come
And that God's Will would be Done

Like a Cancer

Man was Made from Dust
From God, He was Given a Soul
Living by God's Standard, a Must
Making Heaven His Final Goal

For Man's Sin, Even the Innocent Pay
The Little Ones whom We all Love
Just to Hold On that I do Pray
And Trust Our Father from Above

Life at Times Seems like a Cancer
Full of Trouble, No Hope and No Cure
From Our Father Above, only He can Answer
Until He does We have to Endure

Praise the Lord for Each Day and Night
For a Beautiful Trouble Free World
That Our Family is Well, Healthy and Bright
As We Watch a Bright New Morning Unfurl

Love the Lord, Our Heavenly King
For Being There when in Need
For the Blessings He Does Bring
And the Many Souls that He Does Feed

ANGEL'S REFLECTION

Many Times We call Out Thy Name
Hoping for an Answer to a Prayer
Other's Troubles put Ours to Shame
So Dear Lord, Keep them in Thy Care

So I Thank You for Many Blessings
For Myself and My Family Too
Will Man's Trouble Ever Lessen?
Only if We Give Our Life to You

I Know Not, How Our Trouble will End
Or if We'll Be Here to See it Through
But Just Knowing that I have You for a Friend
Thank You Lord, for just Being You

Trouble Seems to Be Man's Name
For Through History there has been No End
The Years and Months are the Same
Thank You Lord for Being Our Friend

We can Talk to Him Whenever We Please
For He is Always there to Advise and Listen
We Don't have to Beg or Get on Our Knees
All He Asks is to Love Him, Jew or Christian

I Pray I Go Quick

Lord How Long must We Wait
To Enter Our Kingdom on High?
Will Our Key Open the Golden Gate
When the Time Comes for Us to Die?

The World Seems to Be in a Mess
With Misery and Trouble all Around
For the Poor there is Never No Rest
But a Place for Them in Heaven will Be Found

There are Earthquakes and Floods Galore
And the Drought is Terrible to Behold
We've had Rain, but Need Some More
For the Crops are Soon to be Ready and Sold

Death will Come as a Thief at Night
And No one will Know Where or When
I Pray God is There to put Out the Light
And Forgive Us if We've Sinned

I Pray that I shall go Quick
And not Burden Anyone on Earth
But Pray Help Me while I'm Sick
Save for Me a Special Birth

ANGEL'S REFLECTION

I've not had Much in this Life
But there are Others Worse than I
There has been Trouble and Strife
  Forgive Me Lord, for I Did Try

I Leave My Love

From this World One Day I'll Leave
And Only the Good Lord knows When
I Pray my Soul He will Receive
For the Thread of Life is Very Thin

I want no Tubes, Pumps, or Artificial Means
For Life is in Our Good Lord's Hands
An Hour or Minute an Eternity it Seems
But Life will End at Our Lord's Command

No Visitation or Flowers Please
And to Our Lord's House for one Last Mass
We Know Life on Earth will Cease
Into another World We shall Pass

Give my Eyes, so Someone might See
For Our World is Beautiful to Behold
My Heart, that in Our Lord, Someone will Believe
And Lungs, before My Body gets Cold

And Anything else that Anyone Needs
I Haven't Given this World as Much as I've Got
Perhaps this Will Be My One Good Deed
For My Possessions are not an Awful Lot

My Treasures of this World are not Much
A Few Pieces of Jewelry made of Gold
Furniture Refinished by Dad's Loving Touch
A Dresser and Pie Safe that's Pretty Old

To My Family I Leave My Love
But Do Not Shed any Tears for Me
Look at the Beauty of the Heavens Above
Trust in God and in Him Believe

No Fancy Casket

I do Not know about Tomorrow Morning
Or if I'll be Able to Say My Goodbye
For Death does Come without Warning
I'll get my Wishes Down or I'll Surely Try

No Visitation, Except the Day I'm Buried
Just Before I go Back to My Church
Which I Dearly Love and Where I was Married
No Fancy Casket just a Plain one of Birch

Dressed as if Going to Church or Town
And I would Dress to Meet My Lord
Don't feel Unhappy or Down
Willing to Go of My Own Accord

Just Don't try to Bring Me Back
For I'm going to a Better Place than This
I Love You All, a saying I Truly Lack
Take Care of One Another and give from Me a Kiss

Made in the USA
Columbia, SC
09 June 2025